D0567922

LANDMARK TOP TENS

The World's Most Amazing
Bridges

Michael Hurley

Chicago, Illinois

www.heinemannraintree.com
Visit our website to find out more information about Heinemann-Raintree books.

To order:

☎ Phone 888-454-2279

🖥 Visit www.heinemannraintree.com to browse our catalog and order online.

Customer Service: 888-454-2279
Visit our website at www.heinemannraintree.com

Edited by Megan Cotugno and Vaarunika Dharmapala
Designed by Victoria Allen
Picture research by Hannah Taylor and Ruth Blair
Original illustrations © Capstone Global Library Ltd (2011)
Production by Camilla Crask
Originated by Capstone Global Library Ltd
Printed in China by CTPS

15 14 13 12
10 9 8 7 6 5 4

Library of Congress Cataloging-in-Publication Data
Hurley, Michael, 1979-
   The world's most amazing bridges / Michael Hurley.—1st ed.
      p. cm.—(Landmark top tens)
   Includes bibliographical references and index.
   ISBN 978-1-4109-4238-8 (hc)—ISBN 978-1-4109-4249-4
(pb) 1. Bridges—Juvenile literature. I. Title.
TG148.H87 2012
624.2—dc22   2010038398

5201 6457 6/13

Acknowledgments
The author and publishers are grateful to the following for permission to reproduce copyright material: Alamy Images p. 21 (© Pacific Press Service); Corbis pp. 8 (Bettmann), 11 (Ryan Pyle); Getty Images p. 20 (AFP); iStockphoto p. 17 (© Brasil2); Photolibrary pp. 13 (Imagebroker), 26 (age fotostock/Andoni Canela), 4–5, 7, 10, 12, 19, 23; Shutterstock pp. 6 (© PHB.cz/Richard Semik), 9 (© Vacclav), 14 (© iofoto), 15 (© Debra James), 18 (© Darrenp), 22 (© Dan Breckwoldt), 25 (© Stas Volik), 24 (© Bryce Newell), 27 (© Lawrence Wee); © Wilfredo R. Rodriguez H. p. 16.

Cover photograph of Sydney Harbour Bridge reproduced with permission of Shutterstock (© HomeStudio).

We would like to thank Daniel Block for his invaluable help in the preparation of this book.

Every effort has been made to contact copyright holders of material reproduced in this book. Any omissions will be rectified in subsequent printings if notice is given to the publisher.

Contents

Some words are printed in bold, **like this**. You can find out what they mean in the glossary.

Bridges

Bridges can be found in every country in the world. Some of them are amazing because they are very old. Others are amazing because of the way they look.

People have been building bridges for more than a thousand years. Bridges have been built for many different reasons. The earliest bridges were very simple designs. They were built to connect two places that were separated by water or land that was difficult to cross.

This bridge in France is called an **aqueduct**. It was built by the Romans about 2,000 years ago to carry water from one place to another.

Modern bridges

The span (length) and the height of bridges have increased over time. New building techniques and building materials have made this possible. Modern bridges are often built to make it quicker and easier to travel by car or train. Some modern bridges have been built to connect two countries over large bodies of water. These bridges mean that boat trips that may have taken hours in the past have been replaced by car trips that take only a fraction of the time.

Millau Viaduct

The Millau **Viaduct** is an amazing modern bridge in France. It is 1.5 miles (2.46 kilometers) long and it connects two areas that are separated by a huge **gorge**. The Millau Viaduct is the world's tallest bridge, at more than 804 feet (245 meters) off the ground at its highest point. The roadway of the bridge rests on seven **piers**. The piers are all different heights.

Tourists come from all over the world to see this spectacular bridge.

Built To Last

The Millau Viaduct was designed to be able to withstand wind speeds of up to 100 miles (160 kilometers) per hour.

The Millau Viaduct cost $516 million to build. It costs $8 to drive a car across the bridge.

Millau Viaduct
Location: Millau, France
Length: 1.5 miles (2.46 kilometers)
That's Amazing!
This bridge is taller than the Eiffel Tower in Paris!

Cable-stayed bridge

The Millau Viaduct is the world's longest cable-stayed bridge. A cable-stayed bridge has towers with cables that connect to a road. These cables support the weight of the road.

Brooklyn Bridge

Brooklyn Bridge is a famous landmark in New York City. The bridge was built during a time of massive growth for the city. It was built across the East River to connect Brooklyn, a New York City borough, to Manhattan Island. It was completed in 1883 after 14 years of construction.

This photograph of the Brooklyn Bridge was taken in 1877, halfway through its construction.

Dynamite

Dynamite was used for the first time (in bridge building) during the construction of Brooklyn Bridge.

When it was completed in 1884, the Brooklyn Bridge was the longest suspension bridge in the world.

Brooklyn Bridge

Location: New York City, New York, USA

Length: 1.17 miles (1.9 kilometers)

That's Amazing!

When this bridge was completed, a group of animals, including 21 elephants, was taken across it to prove that it was strong!

Suspension bridge

The Brooklyn Bridge is a suspension bridge. This means that its weight is suspended by strong cables. There are two giant **granite** towers standing 276 feet (84 meters) tall at either end of the bridge. Two long cables connect the towers across the river. Smaller cables support the weight of the road.

Lupu Bridge

The Lupu Bridge, which stretches across the Huangpu River in Shanghai, China, is the second longest arch bridge in the world. The bridge is 2.4 miles (3.9 kilometers) long, and the arch is 1,804 feet (550 meters) high. It was one of the world's most complicated bridges to build. Three different kinds of bridge design were used: arch, cable-stayed, and suspension.

Record-setting Bridge

The 16 horizontal staying cables used in the bridge are the longest in the world at 2,493 feet (760 meters). They are also the heaviest at 110 tons each.

The Lupu Bridge was opened in 2003. It cost more than $300 million to build.

Amazing city views

The bridge has a public observation deck at the top. It takes 367 steps to reach it, so you need to be in good shape! On the top deck there is an amazing view across Shanghai.

A tourist makes her way up to the Lupu Bridge observation deck.

Lupu Bridge
Location: Shanghai, China
Length: 2.4 miles (3.9 kilometers)
That's Amazing!
The arch on this bridge is the tallest in the world!

Oresund Bridge

The Oresund Bridge is a roadway and railway bridge that connects Denmark and Sweden across the Oresund Strait. At 10 miles (16 kilometers) long, it is the longest roadway bridge in Europe. The bridge structure is made up of a main bridge and two smaller bridges. The span of the main bridge is the longest for any cable-stayed bridge in the world that carries both cars and trains.

Oresund Bridge
Location: Denmark and Sweden
Length: 10 miles (16 kilometers)
That's Amazing!
More than 60,000 people use the bridge each day.

The Oresund Bridge has a roadway at the top, with a train track running beneath it.

At the middle span of the bridge the cables take the weight of the road.

Connecting two countries

The bridge is always very busy with **commuters** crossing the Oresund Strait. Every year 6 million vehicles and 8 million train passengers use the bridge to travel between Sweden and Denmark. The boat trip takes 45 minutes. By using the Oresund Bridge you can get across by car in just 10 minutes!

Sydney Harbour Bridge

The Sydney Harbour Bridge is a steel arch bridge. It is one of the most famous landmarks in Australia.

The bridge crosses Sydney Harbour and gives a spectacular view of the famous Sydney Opera House.

Sydney Harbour Bridge

Location: Sydney, Australia

Length: 0.7 mile (1.2 kilometers)

That's Amazing!

This bridge is affected by rust and has to be painted regularly. It takes 7,925 gallons (30,000 liters) of paint to cover the whole bridge!

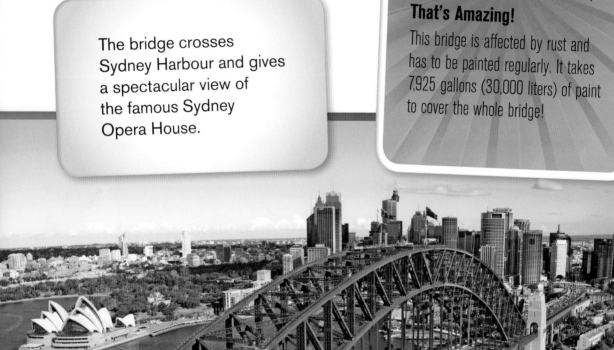

People can climb up to an observation deck on the bridge.

Very wide bridge

Sydney Harbour Bridge took six years to build and was completed in 1932. It is the widest single-span bridge in the world, at 161 feet (49 meters) wide. The bridge contains more than 6 million rivets that were put in by hand. Rivets are small metal bolts used to join two pieces of metal.

Expanding in the Heat

Because of the high temperatures in Australia, this bridge was built with huge hinges at each end. These allow the bridge to expand in the heat of the Sun.

General Rafael Urdaneta Bridge

The General Rafael Urdaneta Bridge in Venezuela is the longest bridge in South America. The bridge stretches across Lake Maracaibo at the narrowest point. When it was built, the bridge cut the amount of time it took to cross from one side of the lake to the other. It used to take two hours by boat. Now it only takes a few minutes by car.

Collision!

In 1964 part of the bridge was damaged after a ship ran into it.

The bridge took five years to build and was completed in 1962.

Until the bridge was built, the province of Maracaibo was isolated from the rest of Venezuela for nearly 390 years.

General Rafael Urdaneta Bridge

Location: Maracaibo, Venezuela

Length: 5.4 miles (8.7 kilometers)

That's Amazing!

This is the longest concrete bridge in the world!

War hero

The bridge is named after General Rafael Urdaneta. He was a hero in the Venezuelan War of Independence (1811–21). The war ended 300 years of Spanish control, and Venezuela became a **republic**.

Bloukrans Bridge

The Bloukrans Bridge is the highest and largest bridge in South Africa. This amazing looking bridge is the largest single-span concrete arch bridge in the world. It is also the third-highest bridge of its kind in the world.

Bloukrans Bridge

Location: Nature Valley, South Africa

Length: 892 feet (272 meters)

That's Amazing!

Thousands of people bungee jump from this bridge every year!

Tourists come to see the spectacular views of the South African landscape from the bridge.

Nature Valley

The bridge spans a **gorge** in Nature Valley, which is one of the most beautiful places in the world. Tourists come from far and wide to visit this area. The bridge is also very popular with people who are looking for an **adrenalin** rush! People can take a **bungee jump** from the bridge.

Record Breaker

The Bloukrans Bridge currently holds the record for the highest bungee jump in the world: 708 feet (216 meters).

Akashi-Kaikyo Bridge

The Akashi-Kaikyo Bridge in Japan is the longest and tallest suspension bridge in the world. When it was built in 1998 it was the most expensive bridge in the world to build. It cost $5.1 billion. Japan is made up of four islands. The Akashi-Kaikyo Bridge was built to connect the islands of Honshu and Shikoku.

Tourist Parks

The Akashi-Kaikyo Bridge is a very popular destination for tourists. Two parks were created near this stunning bridge so that people can view it.

The Akashi-Kaikyo bridge towers are the highest in the world, at 928 feet (283 meters).

In 1995 a strong earthquake hit Kobe in Japan. A huge amount of damage was caused to roads and bridges.

Akashi-Kaikyo Bridge
Location: Kobe, Japan
Length: 2.42 miles (3.9 kilometers)
That's Amazing!
The cables used on this suspension bridge are long enough to circle the Earth seven and a half times!

Very strong bridge

Japan is located in an area of the world that is often affected by earthquakes. The Akashi-Kaikyo Bridge was built to be able to cope with an earthquake of up to 8.5 on the **Richter scale**.

Tower Bridge

Tower Bridge spans the River Thames in London. It is one of the oldest and most famous bridges in the world. The bridge was constructed out of steel and stone. The two stone towers in the central part of the bridge are 200 feet (61 meters) tall. Tower Bridge was built for both pedestrians and vehicles. A road runs across the bottom level of the bridge, while pedestrians use two glass-covered **walkways** that stretch between the two towers.

Crossing The River

There are many bridges that stretch across the River Thames in London. Tower Bridge is the only one with a moveable roadway.

Incredible sight

The most amazing thing about Tower Bridge is that it can raise the roadway to allow boats to travel beneath it. Tower Bridge was completed in 1894. The bridge was built to ease the traffic problems in London at the time.

Tower Bridge

Location: London, United Kingdom

Length: 880 feet (268 meters)

That's Amazing!

In 1952 a London bus had to jump the gap in the bridge after it started to rise!

Tower Bridge in action! The roadway is raised to allow boats to continue along the river.

Golden Gate Bridge

The Golden Gate Bridge in San Francisco is one of the most famous bridges in the world. The bridge is named after the Golden Gate Strait. This body of water is the entrance to San Francisco Bay from the Pacific Ocean.

Golden Gate Bridge

Location: San Francisco, California, USA

Length: 1.7 miles (2.7 kilometers)

That's Amazing!

More than 1.8 billion vehicles have crossed this bridge since it was built!

Sometimes, heavy fog in the Golden Gate Strait means that you cannot actually see the bridge!

Safety Net

A huge net was put under the Golden Gate Bridge when it was being built. This net saved the lives of 19 construction workers.

The Golden Gate Bridge is a popular tourist attraction.

Whose idea was it?

The idea for a bridge stretching across the Golden Gate Strait was first thought of in 1869 by Emperor Norton, a well-known resident of San Francisco. Construction of the bridge did not start until 64 years later. The bridge was opened to the public in 1937.

The Future of Bridges

There are still a lot of places in the world that need bridges to be built, for example to speed up the transportation of goods.

Spanning the Bering Strait

One of the places where the construction of a bridge is being considered is between Russia and Alaska. This bridge would need to stretch across the Bering Strait. However, in the winter much of the water turns to ice. This would mean that construction work could only take place during the summer.

A bridge across the icy waters of the Bering Strait would take a long time to build, and it would cost a lot of money.

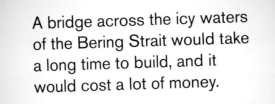

The Henderson Waves Bridge in Singapore is a very unusual looking pedestrian bridge.

New bridge technology

As technology improves, more and more spectacular looking bridges are being built. Some new pedestrian bridges look like pieces of art. The bridges of the future will not only serve a purpose, but they will also look amazing!

Bridges Facts and Figures

There are bridges all over the world. There are long bridges that stretch across huge bodies of water. There are also bridges that were built over 100 years ago. Which bridge do you think is the most amazing?

Millau Viaduct
Location: Millau, France
Length: 1.5 miles (2.46 kilometers)
That's Amazing!
This bridge is taller than the Eiffel Tower in Paris!

Brooklyn Bridge
Location: New York City, New York, USA
Length: 1.17 miles (1.9 kilometers)
That's Amazing!
When this bridge was completed, a group of animals, including 21 elephants, was taken across it to prove that it was strong!

Lupu Bridge
Location: Shanghai, China
Length: 2.4 miles (3.9 kilometers)
That's Amazing!
The arch on this bridge is the tallest in the world!

Oresund Bridge
Location: Denmark and Sweden
Length: 10 miles (16 kilometers)
That's Amazing!
More than 60,000 people use the bridge each day.

Sydney Harbour Bridge

Location: Sydney, Australia

Length: 0.7 mile (1.2 kilometers)

That's Amazing!

This bridge is affected by rust and has to be painted regularly. It takes 7,925 gallons (30,000 liters) of paint to cover the whole bridge!

General Rafael Urdaneta Bridge

Location: Maracaibo, Venezuela

Length: 5.4 miles (8.7 kilometers)

That's Amazing!

This is the longest concrete bridge in the world!

Bloukrans Bridge

Location: Nature Valley, South Africa

Length: 892 feet (272 meters)

That's Amazing!

Thousands of people bungee jump from this bridge every year!

Akashi-Kaikyo Bridge

Location: Kobe, Japan

Length: 2.42 miles (3.9 kilometers)

That's Amazing!

The cables used on this suspension bridge are long enough to circle the Earth seven and a half times!

Tower Bridge

Location: London, United Kingdom

Length: 880 feet (268 meters)

That's Amazing!

In 1952 a London bus had to jump the gap in the bridge after it started to rise!

Golden Gate Bridge

Location: San Francisco, California, USA

Length: 1.7 miles (2.7 kilometers)

That's Amazing!

More than 1.8 billion vehicles have crossed this bridge since it was built!

Glossary

adrenalin hormone that is created in the body. It raises the heart rate and blood pressure when the body is in danger.

aqueduct bridge that carries water across a valley

bungee jump sport of jumping from a bridge or other high place attached to a long elastic rope

commuter person who travels to and from work

dynamite explosive material

gorge narrow valley between hills or mountains

granite very hard rock often used as a building material

pier solid support designed to take a heavy weight

republic state that has an elected or nominated president instead of a queen or king

Richter scale scale used to measure the power of earthquakes

viaduct bridge that takes a railway over a road, river, or valley

walkway passage or path for walking on

Find Out More

Books

Graham, Ian. *Fabulous Bridges.* Mankato, Minn.: Amicus, 2011.

Mitchell, Susan K. *The Longest Bridges.* Milwaukee, Wis.: Gareth Stevens, 2008.

Phillips, Cynthia. *Bridges and Spans.* Armonk, NY: Sharpe Focus, 2009.

Ratliff, Thomas M. *You Wouldn't Want to Work on the Brooklyn Bridge!* New York, NY: Franklin Watts, 2009.

Wolny, Phillip. *High Risk Construction Work: Life Building Skyscrapers, Bridges, and Tunnels.* New York, NY: Rosen, 2009.

Websites

http://kids.yahoo.com
Search for "bridges," "stadiums," and "skyscrapers" to find interesting facts as well as links to other useful sites.

http://www.pbs.org/wgbh/buildingbig
Explore large structures and what it takes to build them, including skyscrapers and bridges.

Index